Hello, I'm a
PANGOLIN

by Hayley & John Rocco

putnam

G. P. PUTNAM'S SONS

Oh, hello.

I didn't know you were there.

I mostly keep to myself, but if

you want to know, I'm a pangolin.

Humans often confuse me with the anteater or the armadillo, and some people even say I look like an artichoke with a face.

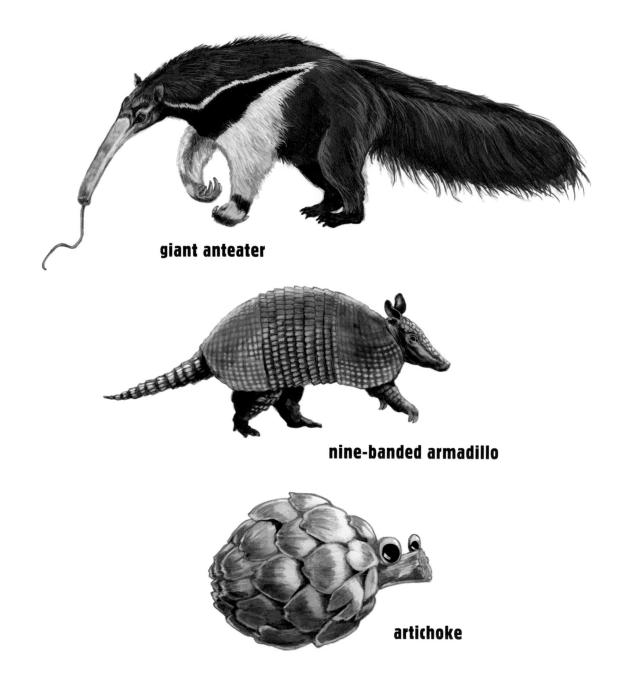

giant anteater

nine-banded armadillo

artichoke

But I am not any of those things.

Actually, my closest relatives
are bears and cats.

I walk on my hind legs (like a T. rex!), and I have large claws that I use for digging holes, called burrows, to sleep in.

Where do
you sleep?

My claws are also useful for digging up tasty snacks. Termites and ants are my favorite. My super-sticky tongue is as long as my entire body. With every flick of it, I grab oodles of them.

And guess what—I eat about 20,000 in a single day. Yum!

I close my ears and nostrils up tight
to keep these critters from crawling
inside and biting me while I eat.

I recently discovered that I am the only
warm-blooded animal with scales.
Can you imagine seeing a bear or a cat
with scales? I haven't counted them all,
but I was told I have almost four hundred.

Can you count them?

Believe it or not, my scales are made
of the same stuff as your fingernails.

How many fingernails do you have?

I can use my scales as armor
if I need to protect myself.

When I'm scared, I simply roll
into a tight ball, like this!

Not even the sharp teeth or claws of a lion
can break through my armor.

But if they won't leave me alone, a swish
of my tail with its super-sharp scales
usually does the trick.

There are eight different types of pangolins in the world, and they can be found in Asia and Africa.

ASIAN PANGOLINS

Chinese pangolin

Philippine pangolin

Sunda pangolin

Indian pangolin

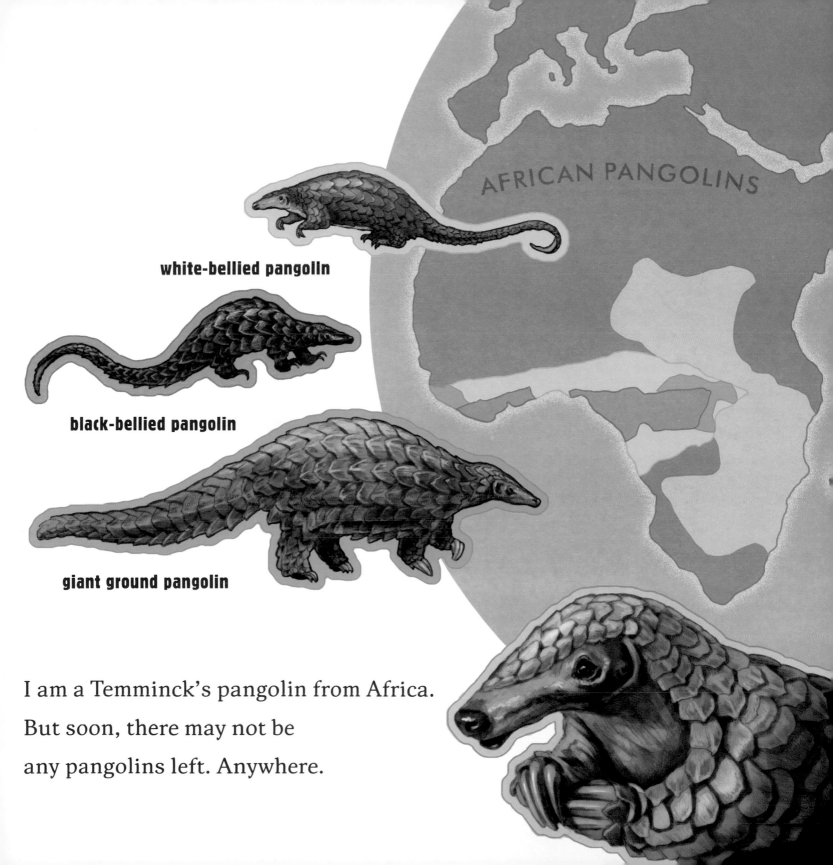

AFRICAN PANGOLINS

white-bellied pangolin

black-bellied pangolin

giant ground pangolin

I am a Temminck's pangolin from Africa.
But soon, there may not be
any pangolins left. Anywhere.

One of the biggest reasons is that some humans
have been stealing us from our homes.

They do this because they want our scales. They believe our scales can heal people.

So they turn our scales into medicine. But like I said before, our scales are made of the exact same thing as your fingernails.

Are your fingernails medicine? Nope. And neither are my scales.

We can give birth to only one baby a year,
so the number of pangolins in the world
is getting smaller and smaller.

Luckily, some humans want to make sure
we don't disappear forever. They watch over us
in the wild to make sure we're not stolen.

They also educate people
about us, and that helps as well.

With their help—and maybe yours, too—we pangolins
can be around for a long time to come.

Okay, well, there's oodles more ants
to eat, so we'd better get going.
But I hope to see you again soon!

A little more about pangolins:

- The name *pangolin* comes from the Malay word *pĕngguling*, meaning "roller."

- Pangolins are critical to the environments they live in, as they regulate insect populations—each one consumes up to 70 million ants and termites per year.

- Though pangolins will dig their own burrows if necessary, they are also opportunistic home hunters. This means, if they find an empty aardvark or porcupine burrow, they'll simply move in instead of digging their own.

- Pangolins have poor eyesight and rely on their excellent sense of smell and hearing to locate their prey.

- Pangolins do not have teeth, but they have a muscular stomach similar to a bird's gizzard. They swallow small amounts of sand while feeding, which helps them grind up their food.

- Pangolins will not eat in captivity, so rescuers must take them for walks to places where plenty of termites and ants live.

- The smallest pangolins (black-bellied) weigh about four pounds, whereas the largest (giant ground) can weigh over seventy pounds.

- Scientists haven't studied the life expectancy of a pangolin yet, but they believe the Temminck's pangolin may live 20 to 22 years in the wild and the giant pangolin anywhere from 30 to 40 years.

- While pangolins can have a baby once a year, recent research shows it's more likely they have one baby every two years. When it is first born, the pup will remain in the burrow while its mother leaves to feed. Once it is strong enough, the pup will ride on its mother's tail for up to three months. It will stay with its mother for five to eight months before venturing out on its own.

- A pangolin's scales make up about 20 percent of its body weight.

- If a predator approaches a mother and her pup, she will wrap herself around the baby tightly until the threat is gone.

- Pangolins roll around in other animals' poop (for example, rhino or zebra) and pee on themselves to cool down. They also enjoy rolling in the mud, but scientists aren't sure whether they do this to get rid of parasites or simply because they like doing it.

- Pangolins can swim and enjoy being in the water.

- Using their claws and strong prehensile tail—a tail that can grasp and hold on to things—most species make great climbers. Only two out of the eight types of pangolin cannot climb trees: the Temminck's pangolin and the giant ground pangolin.

- Pangolins have a top speed of three miles per hour.

- Pangolins can contract infections like pneumonia, which is caused by the stress of being held captive by humans for too long. When pangolins are rescued from poachers, their health is tracked by veterinarians to ensure they are as strong and healthy as possible before being released back into the wild to live on their own.

Why are pangolins endangered?

Pangolins are the most illegally trafficked mammal on Earth, even though all eight pangolin species are protected under national and international laws. Up to 200,000 pangolins are poached—or taken illegally—from the wild every year for not only their scales, but also their meat, which is a delicacy in some parts of the world. When pangolins are rescued, conservationists attach telemetry tags—a type of tracking device—to their scales, which help them locate the animals in the wild, track their behavior, and ensure they're safe. They also report and capture poachers who are taking pangolins to sell into the illegal wildlife trade.

Organizations working to help pangolins:

African Pangolin Working Group: AfricanPangolin.org
Wild Tomorrow: WildTomorrow.org
Save Vietnam's Wildlife: SVW.vn

Temminck's pangolin

©Shannon Wild

For more information about pangolins and how you can help them, visit
MeetTheWildThings.com

For Tori Gray. Thank you for introducing us to the Temminck's pangolin. —H.R. & J.R.

HAYLEY AND JOHN ROCCO are both ambassadors for Wild Tomorrow, a nonprofit focused on conservation and rewilding South Africa. They are the author and illustrator team behind the picture book *Wild Places: The Life of Naturalist David Attenborough*. John is also the #1 *New York Times* bestselling illustrator of many acclaimed books for children, some of which he also wrote, including *Blackout*, the recipient of a Caldecott Honor, and *How We Got to the Moon*, which received a Sibert Honor and was longlisted for the National Book Award. Learn more at MeetTheWildThings.com.

ACKNOWLEDGMENTS Our immense gratitude goes to the wildlife rehabilitators, veterinarians, and pangolin conservation experts working in the field to protect these fascinating and beautiful creatures, including Nicci Wright, wildlife rehabilitation specialist, co-chair of the African Pangolin Working Group, wildlife project manager for the Humane Society International/Africa, co-founder of the Johannesburg Wildlife Veterinary Hospital, and member of the International Union for Conservation of Nature Pangolin Specialist Group; and Charli Pretorius, ecologist for &Beyond Phinda Private Game Reserve and Munywana Conservancy. And our extra-special thanks to Tori Gray and Wild Tomorrow for connecting us with these inspiring conservationists working hard to save pangolins every day.

G. P. PUTNAM'S SONS | An imprint of Penguin Random House LLC, New York
First published in the United States of America by G. P. Putnam's Sons, an imprint of Penguin Random House LLC, 2024

Text copyright © 2024 by Hayley Rocco | Illustrations copyright © 2024 by John Rocco

Library of Congress Cataloging-in-Publication Data | Names: Rocco, Hayley, author. | Rocco, John, illustrator. | Title: Hello, I'm a pangolin / written by Hayley Rocco; illustrated by John Rocco. | Other titles: Hello, I am a pangolin | Description: New York: G. P. Putnam's Sons, 2024. | Series: Meet the wild things; 2
Summary: "An introduction to the unique characteristics of the pangolin"—Provided by publisher. | Identifiers: LCCN 2023009827 (print)
LCCN 2023009828 (ebook) | ISBN 9780593618158 (hardcover) | ISBN 9780593618172 (kindle edition) | ISBN 9780593618165 (ebook)
Subjects: LCSH: Pangolins—Juvenile literature. | Classification: LCC QL737.P5 R63 2024 (print) | LCC QL737.P5 (ebook) | DDC 599.3/1—dc23/eng/20230308
LC record available at https://lccn.loc.gov/2023009827 | LC ebook record available at https://lccn.loc.gov/2023009828

ISBN 9780593618158 | 10 9 8 7 6 5 4 3 2 1
Manufactured in China | TOPL

Design by Nicole Rheingans | Text set in Narevik | The art was created with pencil, watercolor, and digital color.
The publisher does not have any control over and does not assume any responsibility for author or third-party websites or their content.